COMMENDATIONS

OF

FIRST DIVISION

American
Expeditionary Forces
1917—1919

France * Germany

"The Commander-in-Chief has noted in this Division a special pride of service and a high state of morale, never broken by hardship nor battle."

G. O. No. 201, G. H. Q., A. E. F., Nov. 19, 1918.

Roster
First Division.

COMMANDERS.

Major General William L. Sibert	June 8, 1917 to Dcc. 14, 1917.
Major General Robert L. Bullard	Dec. 14, 1917 to July 17, 1918.
Major General Charles P. Summerall	July 17, 1918 to Oct. 11, 1918.
Brigadier General F. E. Bamford	Oct. 11, 1918 to Oct. 19, 1918.
Brigadier General Frank Parker	Oct. 19, 1918 to Nov. 20, 1918.
Major General E. F. McGlachlin, Jr.	Nov. 20, 1918 to date.

CHIEFS OF STAFF.

Colonel Frank W. Coe, G.S.	June 8, 1917 to Sept. 2, 1917.
Colonel H. E. Ely, G.S.	Sept. 2, 1917 to Dec. 16, 1917.
Lt. Col. Campbell King, G.S.	Dec. 16, 1917 to Sept. 23, 1918.
Lt. Col. J. N. Greeley, F.A.	Sept. 23, 1918 to Nov. 8, 1918.
Colonel S. O. Fuqua, G.S.	Nov. 8, 1918 to date.

ASSISTANT CHIEFS OF STAFF.

G—1

Lt. Col. G. K. Wilson, G.S.	Jan. 7, 1918 to July 24, 1918.
Lt. Col. P. E. Peabody, G.S.	July 24, 1918 to date.

G—2.

Major Offnere Hope, G.S.	Sept. 5, 1917 to Nov. 19, 1917.
Captain B. H. Connor, Inf. (Acting)	Nov. 20, 1917 to Dec. 13, 1917.
Captain C. P. Noland, Eng.	Dec. 14, 1917 to Feb. 16, 1918.
Lt. Col. W. C. Sherman, G.S.	Feb. 17, 1918 to Aug. 5, 1918.
1st Lt. T. C. Van Cleve, Cav.	Aug. 6, 1918 to Aug. 20, 1918.
Major T. R. Gowenlock, G.S.	Aug. 21, 1918 to Jan. 21, 1919.
Lt. Col. W. R. Scott, Inf.	Jan. 22, 1919 to Feb. 20, 1919.
Captain D. E. Ackers, Inf. (Acting)	Feb. 21, 1919 to May 10, 1919.
Lt. Col. C. C. Allen, G.S.	May 11, 1919 to May 25, 1919.
Lt. Col. W. R. Scott, Inf.	May 26, 1919 to date.

G—3.

Lt. Col. G. C. Marshall, Jr., G.S.	June 8, 1917, to July 16, 1918.
Lt. Col. J. N. Greeley, F.A.	July 17, 1918, to Sept. 23, 1918.
Major B. F. Caffey, Inf.	Sept. 24, 1918, to Oct. 22, 1918.
Lt. Col. W. F. Boswell, G.S.	Oct. 23, 1918, to Jan. 12, 1919.
Major B. D. Edwards, Inf.	Jan. 13, 1919, to Feb. 20, 1919.
Lt. Col. W. R. Scott, Inf.	Feb. 21, 1919, to June 26, 1919.
Lt. Col. W. F. Hoey, Jr., Inf.	June 27, 1919, to date.

BRIGADE COMMANDERS.

FIRST FIELD ARTILLERY BRIGADE.

Brigadier General Peyton C. March Aug. 16, 1917 to Sept. 8, 1917.
Brigadier General W. S. McNair · · Sept. 9, 1917 to Oct. 13, 1917.
Brigadier General G. H. McKinstry Oct. 13, 1917 to Dec. 23, 1917.
Brigadier General C. P. Summerall Dec. 23, 1917 to July 17, 1918.
Colonel L. R. Holbrook · · · · · July 17, 1918 to Aug. 12, 1918.
Brigadier General H. W. Butner · Aug. 12, 1918 to May 15, 1919.
Brigadier General L. J. McNair · · May 15, 1919 to June 18, 1919.
Brigadier General Augustine
          McIntyre June 25, 1919 to date.

FIRST INFANTRY BRIGADE.

Brigadier General Omar Bundy · · June 28, 1917 to Sept. 16, 1917.
Brigadier General George B. Duncan Sept. 16, 1917 to May 6, 1918.
Brigadier General John L. Hines May 6, 1918 to Aug. 25, 1918.
Brigadier General Frank Parker · Aug. 25, 1918 to Oct. 17, 1918.
Colonel H. J. Erickson · · · · · Oct. 17, 1918 to Nov. 22, 1918.
Brigadier General Frank Parker · Nov. 22, 1918 to date.

SECOND INFANTRY BRIGADE.

Brigadier General R. L. Bullard · June 7, 1917 to Dec. 14, 1917.
Brigadier General B. B. Buck · · · Dec. 14, 1917 to Aug. 26, 1918.
Brigadier General F. E. Bamford · Aug. 26, 1918 to Oct. 13, 1918.
Brigadier General G. C. Barnhardt Oct. 13, 1918 to Oct. 26, 1918.
Brigadier General F. C. Marshall Oct. 26, 1918 to June 3, 1919.
Brigadier General F. E. Bamford · June 3, 1919 to date.

REGIMENTAL COMMANDERS.

FIFTH FIELD ARTILLERY REGIMENT.

Colonel Charles T. Menoher · · · July 25, 1916 to Aug. 26, 1917.
Colonel George C. H. Moseley · Aug. 26. 1917 to Oct. 12, 1917.
Colonel Dwight E. Aultman · · · Oct. 12, 1917 to May 2, 1918.
Lt. Col. Maxwell Murray · · · · May 2, 1918 to Aug. 1, 1918.
Lt. Col. John T. Kennedy · · · · Aug. 1, 1918 to Nov. 15, 1918.
Colonel C. L. Corbin · · · · · · · Nov. 15, 1918 to April 3, 1919.
Lt. Col. Newton N. Polk · · · · April 3, 1919 to April 11, 1919.
Colonel Thomas W. Hollyday · · April 11, 1919 to April 30, 1919.
Lt. Col. Newton N. Polk · · · · April 30, 1919 to June 13, 1919.
Colonel D. C. McDonald · · · · June 13, 1919 to date.

SIXTH FIELD ARTILLERY REGIMENT.

Colonel W. S. McNair · · · · · · · Aug. 13, 1917 to Sept. 15, 1917.
Colonel C. C. Pulis · · · · · · · Sept. 15, 1917 to Dec. 1, 1917.
Colonel E. D. Scott · · · · · · · Dec. 1, 1917 to March 1, 1918.
Lt. Col. J. A. Crane · · · · · · · March 1, 1918 to April 30, 1918.
Lt. Col. Cortlandt Parker · · · April 30, 1918 to Aug. 1, 1918.
Major R. B. Austin · · · · · · · Aug. 1, 1918 to Aug. 10, 1918.
Colonel W. H. Dodds Jr. · · · · Aug. 10, 1918 to May 15, 1919.
Lt. Col. Guy R. Malony · · · · · May 15, 1919 to May 23, 1919.
Colonel Nelson E. Margetts · · · May 23, 1919 to date.

SEVENTH FIELD ARTILLERY REGIMENT.

Colonel Samuel D. Sturgis · · · July 17, 1916 to July 1, 1917·
Colonel William L. Kenly · · · · July 1, 1917 to Aug. 24, 1917
Colonel L. R. Holbrook · · · · · Aug. 24, 1917 to July 15, 1918·
Lt. Col. Alfred L. P. Sands · · · July 15, 1918 to Aug. 3, 1918·
Colonel Francis A. Ruggles · · · Aug. 3, 1918 to date.

SIXTEENTH INFANTRY REGIMENT.

Colonel W. H. Allaire · · · · · Aug. 8, 1915 to Aug. 23, 1917.
Major G. D. Freeman · · · · · Aug. 23, 1917 to Sept. 5, 1917.
Colonel F. A. Wilcox · · · · · · Sept. 5, 1917 to Nov. 2, 1917.
Colonel J. L. Hines · · · · · · · Nov. 2, 1917 to May 3, 1918.
Colonel F. E. Bamford · · · · · · May 3, 1918 to Aug. 27, 1918.
Lt. Col. E. R. Coppock · · · · · Aug. 27, 1918 to Oct. 23, 1918.
Colonel W. F. Harrell · · · · · · Oct. 23, 1918 to May 3, 1919.
Lt. Col. H. L. Evans · · · · · · · May 3, 1919 to May 10, 1919,
Lt. Col. C. W. Ryder · · · · · · May 10, 1919 to May 13, 1919.
Colonel W. F. Harrell · · · · · · May 13, 1919 to June 29, 1919.
Major L. R. Boyd · · · · · · · · June 29, 1919 to July 7, 1919.
Colonel W. W. McCammon · · · July 7, 1919 to date.

EIGHTEENTH INFANTRY REGIMENT.

Colonel J. W. McAndrew · · · · June 28, 1917 to July 21, 1917.
Colonel U. G. Alexander · · · · July 21, 1917 to Dec. 30, 1917.
Colonel Frank Parker · · · · · · Dec. 30, 1917 to Aug. 25, 1918.
Colonel C. A. Hunt · · · · · · · Aug. 25, 1918 to May 6, 1919.
Lt. Col. W. F. Hoey, Jr. · · · · May 6, 1919 to May 21, 1919.
Colonel C. A. Hunt · · · · · · · May 21, 1919 to date.

TWENTY-SIXTH INFANTRY REGIMENT.

Colonel George B. Duncan · · · June 7, 1917 to Sep. 1, 1917.
Colonel F. G. Lawton · · · · · · Sept. 1, 1917 to Nov. 28, 1917.
Colonel H. A. Smith · · · · · · · Nov. 28, 1917 to July 22, 1918.
Major B. R. Legge · · · · · · · July 22, 1918 to July 25, 1918.
Lt. Col. W. R. Wheeler · · · · · July 25, 1918 to July 27, 1918.

Colonel J. B. Cullison · · · · · · July 27, 1918 to Sept. 19, 1918.
Colonel H. J. Erickson · · · · · Sept. 19, 1918 to Oct. 25, 1918.
Lt. Col. T. Roosevelt, Jr. · · · · Oct. 25, 1918 to Jan. 3, 1919.
Colonel F. L. Knudsen · · · · · Jan. 3, 1919 to Feb. 15, 1919.
Major L. S. Frasier · · · · · · · Feb. 15, 1919 to Mar. 20, 1919.
Colonel R. A. Brown · · · · · Mar. 20, 1919 to date.

TWENTY-EIGHTH INFANTRY REGIMENT.

Colonel B. B. Buck · · · · · · · June 9, 1917 to Sept. 5, 1917.
Captain J. M. Cullison · · · · · Sept. 5, 1917 to Sept. 12, 1917.
Colonel F. W. Kobbe · · · · · · Sept. 12, 1917 to Dec. 14, 1917.
Colonel Hansen E. Ely · · · · · Dec. 14, 1917 to July 15, 1918.
Colonel C. S. Babcock · · · · · · July 15, 1918 to Aug. 4, 1918.
Colonel G. C. Barnhardt · · · · · Aug. 4, 1918 to Oct. 11, 1918.
Major C. R. Huebner · · · · · · Oct. 11, 1918 to Oct. 30, 1918.
Lt. Col. T. W. Hammond · · · · Oct. 30, 1918 to Dec. 8, 1918.
Major W. J. Tack · · · · · · · · Dec. 8, 1918 to Dec. 13, 1918.
Lt. Col. C. R. Huebner · · · · · · Dec. 13, 1918 to Dec. 17, 1918.
Colonel A. H. Huguet · · · · · · Dec. 17. 1918 to date.

FIRST ENGINEER REGIMENT.

Colonel M. M. Patrick · · · · · · May 15, 1917 to Aug. 27, 1917.
Lt. Col. G. R. Lukesh · · · · · · Aug. 27, 1917 to Oct. 10, 1917.
Colonel L. V. Frazier · · · · · · Oct. 10, 1917 to Feb. 18. 1918.
Colonel F. B. Wilby · · · · · · · Feb. 18, 1918 to Mar. 11, 1918.
Colonel L. V. Frazier · · · · · · Mar. 11, 1918 to Aug. 14, 1918.
Colonel W. G. Caples · · · · · · Aug. 14, 1918 to Sept. 26, 1918.
Colonel F. B. Wilby · · · · · · · Sept. 26, 1918 to Mar. 12, 1919.
Colonel E. J. Atkisson · · · · · · Mar. 12, 1919 to date.

Organizations.

Headquarters First Division.
Headquarters Troop.
1st Infantry Brigade.
16th Infantry.
18th Infantry.
2nd Infantry Brigade.
26th Infantry.
28th Infantry.
1st Machine Gun Battalion
2nd Machine Gun Battalion.
3rd Machine Gun Battalion.
1st Field Artillery Brigade.
5th Field Artillery.
6th Field Artillery.
7th Field Artillery.
1st Trench Mortar Battery.
1st Engineers.
1st Ammunition Train.
1st Mobile Ordnance Repair Shop.
1st Engineer Train.
1st Supply Train.
1st Sanitary Train.
2nd Ambulance Co.
3rd Ambulance Co.
12th Ambulance Co.
13th Ambulance Co.
2nd Field Hospital.
3rd Field Hospital.
12th Field Hospital.
13th Field Hospital.
2nd Field Signal Battalion.
Military Police Co. No. 1.
Machine Shop Truck Units No. 30 and No. 2.
Mobile Surgical Unit No. 2.
Sales Commissary Unit No. 309.
Bakery Unit No. 308.
Laundry Unit No. 314.
Clothing and Bathing Unit No. 319.
Pack Train No. 10.

A TRIBUTE TO THE FIRST AMERICANS KILLED ON THE SOIL OF FRANCE.

November 3, 1917.

"The death of this humble corporal and these privates appeals to us with unwonted grandeur. We will, therefore, ask that the mortal remains of these young men be left here, be left to us forever. We will inscribe on their tombs, 'here lie the first soldiers of the United States to fall on the fields of France for justice and liberty'. The passer-by will stop and uncover his head. The travellers of France, of the Allied countries, of America, the men of heart, who will come to visit our battlefields of Lorraine will go out of their way to come here to bring to these graves the tribute of their respect and gratitude. Corporal Gresham, Private Enright and Private Hay, in the name of France, I thank you."

General Bordeaux.

First Division's Work in the Argonne Offensive

Described by Lieutenant Colonel Frederick Palmer.

In Collier's Weekly for March 29, 1919, occurs the second instalment of a story by Lieut. Colonel Frederick Palmer, during the war attached to the Intelligence Section of the General Staff at General Headquarters, American Expeditionary Forces and during the past 25 years probably the best known war correspondent in the world. His story deals with the second phase of the Meuse-Argonne offensive, and contains an account of the part played by the First Division in that battle.

Extract.

"The first was given the place of honor in the general attack of October 4th, and a place of honor in the Argonne battle was to be costly though glorious".

"Since my return home I have been asked if Belleau Woods was our most brilliant action. One answers: Brilliant in what respect? In battle efficiency? In courage? For at the front we thought of divisions only in the terms of efficiency. . . I should place in even higher esteem than Belleau Woods the drive of the 1st and 2nd Divisions toward Soissons in July and possibly still higher that drive which the 1st was now to make. We had a dozen Belleau Woods in the Argonne."

"The first was a Regular Division, the pioneer of our Divisions in France, the longest trained, but it was not regular in the old sense, being better than regular in my mind, as we have understood the word regular in the past. Many of its young officers were out of the training camps, and the men who had filled the gaps in the ranks had come from the volunteers or the draft in all parts of the country. It was amazing how soon that divisional machine made a recruit a regular."

"I think that possibly when the First Division went into the Argonne battle it was the most efficient American Division that ever wore shoe leather. And Summerall in Command. He had led the First in the drive toward Soissons. He is a leader compounded of all kinds of fighting qualities, a crusader and a calculating tactician, who, some say, can be as gentle as the sweetest natured chaplain, while others say, that he is nothing but brimstone and ruthless determination. The First with

Summerall in command. We knew it would go through. It had always gone through. This was the part cast for the First in the A.E.F. We knew it would not attack in too great density, for that is not being mean and nasty to your enemy. Its battalion commanders would not hesitate in an emergency, and its veteran gunners would roll barrages of fire accurately and steadily in front of the infantry. Where strong points resisted the artillery would be prompt with its blast of destruction to clear the way. "As per schedule" begins the account of this operation,—the coldest prose I have ever read for as hot a piece of work as I have ever seen.

The Germans had a hot reception for the First, but the First expected this. It was due on those heights unless the Germans forgot the art of war. Four new divisions were identified on the First's front on the first day's attack.

Constantly, undaunted by casualties, the Division kept plowing ahead, blasting the enemy's counter-attacks before he could bring enough troops to bear, keeping the initiative in its own hands. There were delays from scorching machine gun fire down the roads and ravines, on the slopes of Hill 240, from gas and shell as well as machine gun fire, delays before machine gun fastnesses that would have baffled inexperienced hands, but no prolonged repulses.

For eight days altogether, the First was fighting steadily, not taking bites but in determined persistent action. . . . When the First came out its losses were over 9000 in killed and wounded. Half of its infantry was out of action. It had paid the price, but it was the price of a vital success. . . . . not only the First but the other divisions which fought through the machine gun nests and underbrush were capable of deeds which make Lookout Mountain appear somewhat less of a battle by comparison than some of us think it was. The First had relieved the pressure on the 77th Division thus helping to extricate the "Lost Battalion", and opened the door, closed by crossfire, for the 28th Division, somewhat beleaguered, but now pressing forward on the other side of the Aire Valley at the forest's edge, to repay the First in kind by helping to relieve it of fire from across the valley, . . ."

Germany's Tribute to the First Division:

Today, Oct. 10, 1918, a captured Colonel of the German Army arrived at our Division cage. He was cold, hungry and broken in spirit. After four years of severe fighting and constant service in his army, he was taken prisoner by the troops of the victorious First Division.

The following is the substance of his remarks:

"I received orders to hold my ground at all costs. The American barrage advanced toward my position and the work of your Artillery was marvellous. The barrage was so dense that it was impossible for us to move out of our dug-outs. Following the barrage closely was the Infantry of the First Division. I saw them forge ahead and I knew that all was lost. All night I remained in my dug-out hoping vainly that something would happen which would permit me to rejoin my army. This morning your troops found me and here I am, after four years of fighting, your prisoner.

Yesterday I knew that the First Division was opposite us and I knew that we would have to fight our hardest of the war. The First Division is wonderful and the German Army knows it. We did not believe that within five years the Americans could develop a division like the First. The work of its Infantry and Artillery is worthy of the best armies of the world."

The above tribute to the First Division comes from one of Germany's seasoned field officers. It is with great pleasure that we learn that even our enemies recognize the courage, valor and efficiency of our troops. The work done by the First Division during the past few days will go down in history as one of the most memorable events which will live in the hearts of the American people in the generations to come.

"Courage, Dash, and Victory is First Division's Record"

Story of American Regulars Who Led the Way to France and whose Casualties of all kinds reached 23,974, including 715 Officers.

By Major General A. W. Greeley
(United States Army. Retired).

There is no Division of the American Expeditionary Forces that has failed to display in the face of the enemy the qualities of courage, discipline and efficiency which are acknowledged attributes of the American Army. It is natural and commendable that war correspondents and local newspapers should loudly proclaim the achievements of the military organizations identified with and formed in their own communities. It would be an injustice to the rank and file of our citizen soldiery if their own sections failed to display pride especially in the combat divisions. Thus New England honors the 26th Division, New York the 27th and 77th, Pennsylvania the 28th, Michigan and Wisconsin the 32nd, Kansas and Missouri the 35th, Ohio the 37th, and the Pacific States the 91st, to mention those of greater losses.

It should be borne in mind, however that, certain organizations are entitled to general recognition for their soldierly merits as they present to the world, by the men of their ranks, a thoroughly homogeneous Army, gathered from all sections and all races, of our composite nation. These are the troops of the so called Regular Army, whose ranks are filled, almost to a man, by volunteers, for sercice only in the great war. It is not generally known that the war casualties of these organizations—battle and disease—have depleted their ranks from 25 to 100 percent of their original personnel. These vast gaps have been filled by draft from the replacement divisions of selected men thus making the Regulars truly national organizations.

That the public may appreciate the fibre and metal of these representative troops formed by such a national consolidation it appears desirable and of timely interest that the achievements of a typical Regular Division should be briefly if somewhat inadequately described. For this purpose the First Division is selected, not that its bravery is superior, its discipline better or its morale higher than marked the others, but, it was the first division to reach France, first to serve in trench warfare, first to fire a hostile shell, first to lose a man, first to capture a prisoner, first to repel a German raid, first to man any independent sector, and first to capture a town (Cantigny) and hold it against all counter-attacks.
— Extract from New York Times of February 9, 1919.

Somervillier Sector.

The First Division entered the Somervillier Sector in Lorraine between October 21st and November 20th, 1917.

Battalions of Infantry and Artillery were grouped with corresponding units of the 18th French Division for instruction in the methods of occupying and holding a sector.

It so happened that the 2nd Battalion of the 16th Infantry was raided by the enemy the first night of its entry into the sector. During this raid the Division sustained its first casualties.

During the occupation of this sector the total casualties amounted to:

        Killed — 13 men;
        Wounded — 1 officer, 18 men;
        Prisoners — 11 men;
        Total — 1 officer, 42 men.

Somervillier Sector.

General Order
No. 67.

Headquarters First Division,
American Expeditionary Forces.
France, November, 23, 1917.

1. The troops of the First Division have completed their first tour of duty at the front. The casualties have been few as was expected in a quiet sector; fourteen killed, thirty-four wounded and eleven captured by the enemy. But the many discomforts, inconveniences and trials always incident to service at the front have been faced in a fine, uncomplaining spirit which speaks well for the soldierly qualities of the men. The Division Commander wishes to congratulate the soldiers of the Division upon their excellent conduct and cheerful demeanor during the past month at the front and particularly during the long, hard weeks of preliminary training in the cold and mud. He believes there are few occasions in the past where American soldiers have worked as hard and have endured as cheerfully so many discomforts and difficulties as have the men of this Division since landing in France.

2. We are now starting on the final period of training. Weather conditions will make it a peculiarly hard and trying one. The Division Commander feels that he can depend on every individual soldier to meet this situation with the same fortitude and resolution that he has heretofore displayed and to do his utmost to bring to a successful and speedy conclusion the preparation of this command to take its place, as a unit, in the first line in a manner to reflect credit and honor upon our country.

Wm. L. Sibert
Major General, U.S.A.
Commanding.

———

Ansauville Sector.

The First Division relieved the First Moroccan Division on January 15th, 1918, in the Ansauville Sector, north of Toul. This sector covered a front of seven and a half kilometers.

A raid was made by the enemy against the Third Battalion of the 18th Infantry on March 1st, 1918. On March 11th the Division made two raids against the enemy.

The Division was relieved between April 3rd and 5th 1918, by the 26th American Division.

During its tour in the Ansauville Sector the Division captured ten prisoners.

1st casualties amounted to:

Killed — 6 officers, 103 men;
Wounded — 31 officers, 398 men;
Missing — 1 officer, 3 men;
Total — 38 officers, 504 men.

Ansauville Sector.

1st Army.
32nd Army Corps.
   Staff
3rd Bureau.
    1030/3.

Headquarters, March 2, 1918.

General Order No. 119.

On the 1st of March, at day break, the enemy pulverized the first line trenches and dugouts occupied by the right of the 18th American Regiment with a heavy fire of minenwerfers and 210's. They then attacked in 6 columns under the protection of a rolling barrage.

All instructions which had been given had been faithfully carried out. The Americans withdrew to the edge of the zone under fire, — then delivered a strong counter-attack.

The Boche realized the force of the American blow; he retreated to his position, leaving on the spot 15 dead (of which 2 were officers) and 4 prisoners.

The troops of the 32nd Army Corps, proud to be fighting by the side of the generous Sons of the Great Republic who have hastened to support France and with her to save the freedom of the world, will understand by this example of superb courage and coolness the full meaning of the promises made by the entry into the conflict of their new brothers-in-arms.

The general commanding the 32nd Army Corps heartily congratulates the 1st American Division and in particular the 3rd Battalion of the 18th Infantry as well as the American Artillery whose precise and opportune action contributed to the success.

Passaga
The General Commanding the 32nd Army Corps.

Headquarters, First Division,
American Expeditionary Forces.
France, March 11, 1918.

From: Division Commander.

To: General C. P. Summerall, Commanding 1st Artillery Brigade.

Subject: Action of Artillery Brigade in Remieres and Richecourt Raids, March 11, 1918.

I wish to express to you and to the officers and men of your command my appreciation of the efficiency of your work in the raids just completed.

The accuracy and effectiveness of the fire of your guns
has enabled the raiding detachments to perform their missions
without interference by the enemy and without the loss of
a man, and has undoubtedly inflicted heavy losses on the
enemy in addition to destroying his fortifications. The
Infantry has been inspired with a great confidence by the
assurance of instant and effective support by the artillery.

Please communicate my congratulations to your command.

(Signed): Robert L. Bullard,
Major General, N.A.

Armee   Au Q.F., 21 Mars 1918.
2nd Corps D'Armee Colonial.
10th Division Coloniale.   Le General de Division, Marchand.
Secteur Postal 167.   Commandant la 10th Division
3rd Bureau.   Coloniale.

Commanding General of the 1st Division:

General Marchand, Commandant of the 10th D.I.C. very
warmly thanks the Artillery of the 1st Division, American E.F.
for the help that it gave on the morning of March 20th
against the raid launched by the enemy east of Apremont.

The American Artillery opened its fire with a rapidity
that is worthy of praise and which is proof of its vigilance
and a warrant of its excellent training and instruction.

A few days ago our artillery had the honor and pride
to work for the 1st Division. Yesterday the American
Artillery honored us with its work. The voice of our guns,
American and French, has sealed in both ways the pact of
union and confidence that is in all of our Allies' and soldiers'
hearts.   (Signed): Marchand.

32e Corps d'Armee.
Etat-Major.   Q.G. le 4 Avril, 1918.
3e Bureau.

Ordre General No. 123.

Au moment ou la 1re Division Americaine part pour
la bataille, les officiers, sous-officiers et les soldats du 32e
Corps d'Armee saluent les frères d'Armes dont ils ont admire
la bravoure.

Ils les felicitent d'avoir a ecrire dans la bataille des
Nations la premiere page de l'Histoire des fils de la grande
Republique venant lutter sur le sol de France pour le triomphe
de la Liberté.

Cette page sera glorieuse.

(Signé): Passaga.
Le General Commandant le 32e. C.A.

32e Corps d'Armee.
Etat-Major.   Q.G., le 4 Avril, 1918.
3e Bureau.

Ordre General No. 123.

As the First American Division leaves for battle, the officers, non-commissioned officers and soldiers of the 32nd Army Corps salute their brothers in arms, whose bravery they have admired.

They congratulate them on being privileged to write in the battle of Nations, the first page in the history of the sons of the great Republic coming to fight on the soil of France for the triumph of Liberty.

This page will be glorious.

(Signed): Passaga
Commanding General
32nd Army Corps.

General Orders   Headquarters 1st Division,
No. 16.   American Expeditionary Forces.
                                 France, April 2, 1918.

1. The Commanding General of the 32nd French Army Corps has expressed in orders his approbation of the conduct of the Division while in this sector.

2. The character of the service which the Division is now about to undertake, however, demands enforcement of a stricter discipline and the maintenance of a higher standard of efficiency than any heretofore required of us.

3. From now on troops of this command will be held at all times to the strictest observation of that rigid discipline, in camp and upon the march, which is essential to their maximum efficiency on the day of battle.

4. This order will be read by all organization commanders to the men of their commands.

By command of Major General Bullard.

Campbell King,
Chief of Staff.

Montdidier
(Cantigny Sector)

The First Division occupied a sector five kilometers south of Montdidier from April 25th, 1918 to July 8th, 1918.

The first American offensive was made by the Division against Cantigny.

Casualties in this sector amounted to:—

Killed — 58 officers, 983 men;
Wounded — 178 officers, 4578 men;
Prisoners — 2 men;
Missing — 2 officers, 30 men;
Total — 238 officers, 5593 men.

Cantigny.

| Memorandum
No. 80. | Headquarters First Division,
American Expeditionary Forces,
France, June 2, 1918. |

The recent operations taken against Cantigny and the immediate hostile reaction therefrom may be considered as now concluded. Future activity which may develop in that direction will initiate a new phase. The German attack in front of this Division upon the day preceding the beginning of the Cantigny operation is so closely allied with that operation and the preparation thereto that it may be considered as one of the incidents therewith.

The Division Commander desires at this time to publish to the officers and men of this command his appreciation of the gallantry and steadiness of the troops who took part in these affairs, either as direct participants or in support thereof.

The moral effects, to flow from this proof of reliability in battle of the American soldiers, far outweighs the direct military importance of the actions themselves.

The Division Commander is glad to feel that the conduct of the officers and men of the Division on these two occasions justifies the high standard that our people expect of the American soldiers who are destined to take part in this great struggle.

By command of Major General Bullard,

Campbell King,
Chief of Staff.

| Memorandum
No. 84. | Headquarters First Division,
American Expeditionary Forces,
France, June 3rd, 1918. |

The following letter from the Corps Commander is published for the information of all concerned:

"The Corps Commander desires to express his gratification over the recent successful operations of the 1st Division and to congratulate your officers and soldiers for their ability to uphold the best traditions of the Army of the United States. Their intrepidity and spirit augur well for the succesful accomplishment of the mission of the A.E.F."

By command of Major General Bullard,

H. K. Loughry,
Major, F.A., Division Adjutant.

General Order   Headquarters, First Division,
   No. 24.   American Expeditionary Forces,
                     France, June 3rd, 1918.

The following has been received by the Division Commander from the Commander-in-Chief and is published for the information of all concerned:

"Please accept my hearty congratulations upon the marked success of the attack made by your Division this morning upon Cantigny. Extend to all concerned my warm appreciation of the splendid spirit displayed and the well-ordered fashion in which the details of the plan were carried out. This engagement, though relatively small, marks a distinct step forward in American participation in the war.

With sincere regards, I remain,

Very cordially yours,
John J. Pershing."

By Command of Major General Bullard
H. K. Loughry.
Major, F. A., Division Adjutant.

The following orders and commendations relate to the work of the Division in the Cantigny Sector:

6e Corps d'Armee.   Au Q.G., le 20 Avril 1918.
   Etat-Major.
No. 3543/1.

Ordre General No. 32.

Par ordre du General commandant le 1re Armee en date du 19 avril courant, la 1re D. I. U. S. est rattachee au 6e Corps a partir de demain 21 avril.

Le 6e Corps est particulierement fier d'accuellir a ses cotes devant l'ennemi, les troupes de la noble Nation Americaine, et il leur souhaite une cordiale bienvenue.

L'union intime des efforts dans la grande lutte que nous soutenons pour la liberte du Monde est le meilleur gage de la Victoire.

Au moment ou la 1re D. I. U. S. va entrer en ligne, je salue ses drapeaux, qui viennent se deployer sur la terre de France.

General Duport.

6e Corps d'Armee
   Etat-Major   Au Q. G. le 20 Avril, 1918.
    No. 3543/1.

Ordre General No. 32.

By an order of the Commanding General of the First Army, dated 19 April, 1918, the First American Division is attached to the 6th Corps, commencing tomorrow 21 April.

The 6th Corps is particularly happy to have beside it
in the face of the enemy, the troops of the noble American
nation, and wish them a cordial welcome.

In the intimate unity of our efforts in the great struggle
which we are carrying on for the freedom of the world, lies
our best chance for Victory.

As the First American Division is entering the lines, I
salute its banners, which are unfurled on the soil of France.

General Duport.

10th Army Corps.   July 4, 1918.
No. 818 C.

General Order.

The General, Officers and Men of the First Division:

Tomorrow the first elements of your Division will depart
from the area of the 10th Army Corps. In four days you
will have left us.

I am still deeply impressed by the celebration of your
"Independence Day" and by the magnificent show I witnessed
this morning in reviewing one of your battalions and saluting
the Star Spangled Banner. I wish to express to you the
regret that I and all the officers and men of the 10th Army
Corps feel at seeing you leave this sector where you have
shed your generous blood and earned your first success.

In this sector the French soldiers are called "The Men
of Grivesnes" and you, Sons of America, we are happy to
call "The Men of Cantigny".

General, Officers and Men of the First Division:

In bidding you farewell I wish you the glorious fortune
which your gallantry deserves. As war may bring us together
again, I do not say, "Adieu" but, "Au revoir".

General Vanderburg,
Commanding the 10th Army Corps.

American Expeditionary Forces.

General Order   France, July 9, 1918.
No. 112.

The Commander-in-Chief desires to record in the
General Orders of the American Expeditionary Forces his
appreciation of the splendid courage, service and sacrifice of
the officers and men of the First Division and the Second
Division of these Forces during the recent operations in which

time these divisions participated and in which the enemy was checked by the resolute defence and counter-offense of the Allied Armies.

These divisions, submitted fully for the first time to all the drastic tests of modern warfare, bore themselves always with fine valor; Their cooperation with the brothers-in-arms of the unified command was prompt and efficient and brought from their Allied comrades many expressions of sincere appreciation.

The conduct of these brave men and that of their fallen comrades who made the supreme sacrifice has established a standard of service and prestige which every division of the American Expeditionary Forces will strive to emulate and preserve.

This order will be read to all organizations at the first assembly formation after its receipt.

By Command of General Pershing.

Official:

James W. McAndrew,
Chief of Staff.

Robert C. Davis,
Adjutant General.

Soissons Offensive.

The First Division, shoulder to shoulder with our Second Division, the First Moroccan Division and the 153rd D. I. French, attacked the enemy south of Soissons from July 18 to 23, 1918. The operations were conducted under the 20th French Army Corps of the 10th French Army.

In the five days of fierce fighting we advanced 11 kilometers, capturing 125 officers, 3375 men, 75:77 mm and 150 mm guns, 300 machine guns, 2500 rifles, 50 mortars and large quantities of small arms and ammunition.

Our losses were:

Killed — 78 officers, 1548 men;
Wounded — 214 officers, 6130 men;
Prisoners — 5 men;
Missing — 390 men;
Total — 292 officers, 8073 men.

The Division was relieved by the 15th (Scottish) Division.

Soissons Offensive.

Headquarters, Third Army Corps.
American Expeditionary Forces,
France, July 21, 1918.

From: Adjutant, 3rd Corps.
To: Commanding General, 1st Division.
Subject: Visit of the Commander-in-Chief.

1. At the close of the third day of heavy fighting our Commander-in-Chief came yesterday to visit the 3rd Corps to manifest his intense interest and pride in the achievements of the 1st and 2nd Divisions. He directed me to assure the officers and men of these Divisions of his admiration for their soldierly qualities and excellent spirit, and his confidence that through the efforts of such troops the defeat of the enemy is certain.

2. Publish these expressions of the Commander-in-Chief to the officers and men of your Division.

By Command of Major General Bullard
H. K. Loughry,
Major, F.A., N.A., Adjutant.

General Order
No. 9.

Headquarters, Third Army Corps,
American Expeditionary Forces,
France, July 23rd, 1918.

On the morning of July 18th, after forty-eight hours of exhausting, continous, almost sleepless movement, the 3rd Army Corps joined battle with the enemy. In your great offensive you stood beside the best Veteran French Troops, our Allies, and sustained, nay, did honor to the name American. Our Allies, your commanders, the Army of the United States and the whole nation are proud and will boast of your deeds and the deeds of those brave men, our beloved comrades, who at your side in the last five days have fallen paying the last sacrifice of soldiers. Now and for the future let us resolve that those our Allies and our people shall not trust in us in vain and, in the words of Lincoln, "That these our comrades shall not have died in vain."

By command of Major General Bullard
A. W. Bjornstad,
Brigadier General, G.S., Chief of Staff.

The following orders and commendations relate to the work of the Division in this battle:

To General Officer Commanding   July 24, 1918.
1st American Division.

I would like, on behalf of all ranks of the 15th (Scottish) Division, to express to you personally, to your staff, and to all our comrades in your splendid Division our most sincere thanks for all that has been done to help us in a difficult situation.

During many instances of "taking over" which we have experienced in the war, we have never received such assistance, and that rendered on the most generous scale.

In spite of its magnificent success in the recent fighting, the 1st American Division must have been feeling the strain of the operations accentuated by heavy casualties, yet, we could discern no symptoms of fatigue when it came to a question of adding to it by making our task easier.

To your Artillery Commander (Colonel Holbrook) and his staff and to the units under his command, our special thanks are due. Without hesitation when you saw our awkward predicament as regards artillery support, the guns of your Division denied themselves relief in order to assist us in an attack. This attack was only partly successful but the artillery support was entirely so.

Without the help of Colonel Mabee and his establishment of ambulance cars I have yn hesitation in saying that at least 400 of our wounded would still be on our hands in this area.

The 15th (Scottish) Division desires me to say that our hope is that we may have opportunity of rendering some slight return to the 1st American Division for all the latter has done for us, and further that we may yet find ourselves shoulder to shoulder defeating the enemy in what we may hope is the final stage of the war.

H. L. Reed

Major General,
Commanding, 15th (Scottish) Division.

General Order   Headquarters, First Division,
   No. 38.   American Expeditionary Forces,
                           France, July 25th, 1918.

The Commanding General wishes to express to the officers and soldiers of this Division his pride in their splendid achievements during the operations of July 18—23. Your magnificent courage and unfaltering fortitude have not only won for you individually the admiration of the Allied Armies, but have written a glorious page in the history of that great country which you represent.

For five long days you have maintained a bitter struggle in one of the world's greatest battles and pushed forward in the face of the enemy's most determined resistance. You would not be denied and you have reached the ultimate objective assigned to you in the battle. You have captured for your own share in the fruits of the victory, 3500 prisoners and 66 cannon. No such brilliant success can be obtained without losses, but the injury you have inflicted upon the enemy is many times greater, and today your spirit is unshaken, your courage high, and you are, even now, ready to repeat the lesson you have taught the enemy.

The Commanding General is proud to command such a Division and he expresses to you again the deep gratitude he feels for the splendid soldierly qualities you have so gloriously proven in the unquestioned crucible of the battle field.

This order will be read to all organizations at the first assembly formation after its receipt.

By command of Major General Summerall,

Campbell King,
Chief of Staff.

G.H.Q.

American Expeditionary Forces.

General Order   France, August 28th, 1918.
No. 143.

It fills me with pride to record in General Orders a tribute to the service and achievements of the First and Third Corps, comprising the 1st, 2nd, 3rd, 4th, 26th, 28th, 32nd, and 42nd Divisions of the American Expeditionary Forces.

You came to the battle field at the crucial hour of the Allied cause. For almost four years the most formidable army the world has as yet seen has pressed its invasion of France, and stood threatening its Capital. At no time had that army been more powerful or menacing than when on July 15th, It struck again to destroy in one great battle the brave men opposed to it and enforce its brutal will upon the world and civilization.

Three days later, in conjunction with our Allies, you counter attacked. The Allied Armies gained a brilliant victory that marks the turning point of the war. You did more than give our brave Allies the support to which as a nation our faith was pledged. You proved that our altruism, our pacific spirit, our sense of justice have not blunted our virility and our courage. You have shown that American initiative and energy are as fit for the test of war as for the pursuits of peace. You have justly won the unstinted praise of our Allies and the eternal gratitude of our countrymen.

We have paid for our successes with the lives of many of our brave comrades. We shall cherish their memory always and claim for our history and literature their bravery, achievements and sacrifice.

This order will be read to all organizations at the first assembly formation after its receipt.

John J. Pershing,
General, Commander-in-Chief.

Official:

Robert C. Davis,
Adjutant General.

Xe Armee

Etat-Major
3e Bureau
No. 862/S

Au Q.G.A., le 30 Julliet 1918.

Ordre General No. 318.

Officiers, Sous-Officiers et Soldats du 3rd U.S.A.C. :

Epaule contre epaule avec vos camarades français, vous vous etes jetes dans la bataille de contre-offensive qui a commencee le 18 Juillet.

Vous y avez couru comme a une fete.

Votre elan magnifique a bouscule l'ennemi surpris et votre tenacite indomptable a arrete le retour offensif de ses divisions fraiches.

Vous vous etes montreles dignes fils de votre grand pays et vous avez fait l'admiration de vos fréres d'armes.

91 canons, 7200 prisonniers, un butin immense, 10 kilometres de terrain reconquis, voila votre part dans le trophée de cette victoire.

En outre, vous avez acquis pleinement le sentiment de votre superiorité sur le barbare, ennemi du genre humain tout entier, contre lequel luttent les enfants de la Liberté.

L'attaquer, c'est le vaincre.

Camarades americains, je vous suis reconnaissant du sang genereusement verse sur le sol de ma patrie.

Je suis Fier de vous avoir commandes en de telles journees et d'avoir combattu avec vous pour la deliverance du monde.

M. Mangin.

Xe Armee
Etat-Major
3e Bureau
No. 862/S.

Au Q.G.A., 30th July, 1918.

Ordre General No. 318.

Officers, Non-Commissioned Officers and Soldiers
of the 3rd United States Army Corps.

Shoulder to shoulder with your French comrades you were thrown into the counter-offensive battle which commenced on the 18th of July.

You rushed into the fight as though to a fete.

Your magnificent courage completely routed a surprised enemy and your indomitable tenacity checked the counter-attacks of his fresh Divisions.

You have shown yourselves worthy Sons of your Great Country and you were admired by your brothers in arms.

91 guns, 7,200 prisoners, immense booty, 10 kilometers of country reconquered; this is your portion of the spoil of this victory.

Furthermore, you have really felt your superiority over the barbarous enemy of the whole human race, against whom the children of Liberty are striving.

To attack him is to vanquish him.

American comrades! I am grateful to you for the blood so generously spilled on the soil of my Country.

I am proud to have commanded you during such days and to have fought with you for the deliverance of the world.

Mangin.

Saizerais Sector.

The First Division entered the Saizerais Sector August 7th, 1918, relieving the 2nd Moroccan Division (French) approximately two kilometers southeast of Pont-a-Mousson. There the strength of the Division was brought to normal.

The 90th Division completed its relief of the Division on the night of August 23—24 1918.

Prisoners captured- 6.
Losses :
Killed — 4 men;
Wounded — 19 men;
Missing — 4 men ;
Total — 27 men.

Saizerais Sector.

VIII Armee.
Etat-Major.
3me Bureau.   Ordre General No. 372.

A partir du 30 Aout 1918, les 1er et 4me C.A.U.S. cessent d'appartenir a la VIII Armee Francaise.

Au moment de remettre au General Commandant la 1re Armee Americaine le commandment de la zone de Toul, le General, Commandant la VIII Armee Française est heureux d'exprimer aux belles Divisions Americaines qui s'y sont succede le temoignage de son entiere satisfaction pour les brillantes qualités militaires dont elles ont constamment fait preuve sur cette partie du front de la VIII Armee.

Toutes ces Divisions qui ont eu a coeur de defeudre leur secteur avec tant d'energie, et dont certaines ont montre un elan irresistible au cours de la recente bataille, assurrent a l'Armee Americaine, sous le haut Commandement de son Chef eminent, les plus brillants succes.

le 30 Aout 1918.

(Signed) General Gerard.

Destinataires: 1ere, 2me, 82me, 89me et 90me, D.I.U.S

8th Army,
    Staff
3rd Bureau.

General Order No. 372.

On the 30th of August, the First and Fourth Army Corps, American E. F., will cease to belong to the 8th French Army.

At the time of passing the command of the Toul Sector to the Commanding General, 1st Army, A.E.F., the Commanding General, 8th French Army, is glad to convey upon the gallant American Divisions, who occupied this sector, his best appreciation of the brilliant soldierly qualities which they displayed on this part of the front.

All these Divisions, who put their whole energy in the defense of the sector, and those among them who displayed the most irresistible daring during the last battle, will, under the high command of their distinguished General, secure for the United States Army the most durable fame.

August 30th, 1918.

General Gerard.

St. Mihiel Offensive.

The First Division as a part of the First American Army participated in the St. Mihiel Offensive, September 12—13, 1918. We advanced fourteen kilometers in nineteen hours. Small elements of the Division advanced nineteen kilometers in thirty-two hours.

Prisoners captured—5 officers, 1190 men.

Material captured—30 : 77 mm. and 150 mm. guns 50 machine guns, 100 rifles, quantities of small arms ammunition, and 3 locomotives.

Our losses amounted to:
Killed—2 officers, 82 men;
Wounded—11 officers, 478 men;
Missing—19 men;
Prisoners—1 man;
Total—13 officers, 580 men.

St. Mihiel.

General Orders
No. 6.

Headquarters, Fourth Army Corps.
September 13th, 1918.

1. The Fourth Corps has defeated the enemy and driven him back on the whole Corps front. All objectives were reached ahead of the time prescribed, a large number of prisoners and a considerable amount of booty captured. The rapid advance of the Corps, in conjunction with the action of the elements of the First Army, rendered the St. Mihiel salient untenable to the enemy, who has retreated.

2. The greatest obstacle to the advance was thought to be the enemy's wire, which presented a problem that caused anxiety to all concerned. The Corps Commander desires to express in particular his admiration of the skill shown by the small groups in the advance battalions and their commanders in crossing the hostile wire, and, in general, to express his appreciation of the high spirit and daring shown by the troops, and the rapidity and efficiency with which the operation was conducted.

By command of Major General Dickman:

Steward Heintzelman,
Colonel, General Staff.
Chief of Staff.

Washington, September 14, 1918.

General John J. Pershing,
American Expeditionary Forces.
France.

Accept my warmest congratulations on the brilliant achievements of the Army under your command. The boys have done what we expected of them and done it in the way we most admire. We are deeply proud of them and of their chief. Please convey to all concerned my grateful and affectionate thanks.

(Signed) Woodrow Wilson.

September 14, 1918.

General Pershing, Headquarters,
American Expeditionary Forces,
France.

All ranks of the British Armies in France welcome with unbounded admiration and pleasure the victory which has attended the initial offensive of the great American Army under your personal command. I beg you to accept and to convey to all ranks my best congratulations and those of all ranks of the British Armies under my command.

(Signed) Haig.

France, September 14, 1918.

General John J. Pershing.
American Expeditionary Forces,
        France.

My dear General, the First American Army, under your command on the first day, has won a magnificent victory by a maneuver as skillfully prepared as it was valiantly acted. I extend to you, as well as to the officers and troops under your command, my warmest compliments.

(Signed) Marshal Foch.

General Orders
No. 56.

Headquarters, First Division,
American Expeditionary Forces,
France, September 16, 1918.

1. The Division Commander desires to express to the officers and men of the Division his appreciation of their gallant conduct in the recent operation against St. Mihiel salient. In spite of formidable wire entanglements, badly broken terrain and most unfavorable weather, the Division went straight to its objectives on schedule time, speedily overcoming the enemy and driving him back in disorder from his strongly organized positions, capturing many prisoners and much valuable war material. Owing to your skill and courage your own losses have been light and you are today stronger and better prepared than ever to administer another blow to our enemy.

2. As at Soissons, so at St. Mihiel you have gallantly lived up to the best traditions of American manhood and have added another glorious page to the history of our country. The honor of commanding such a division must ever fill with pride the heart of its commander who can confidently look to it to maintain on future battle-fields the splendid record of the past.

C. P. Summerall,
Major General U.S.A.

G.H.Q.
American Expeditionary Forces.

General Orders   France, December 26. 1918.
  No. 238.

It is with soldierly pride that I record in General Orders a tribute to the taking of the St. Mihiel Salient by the First Army.

On September 12, 1918, you delivered the first concerted offensive operation of the American Expeditionary Forces upon difficult terrain against this redoubtable position, immovably held for 4 years, which crumpled before your ably executed advance. Within 24 hours after the commencement of the attack the salient had ceased to exist and you were threatening Metz.

Your divisions, which had never been tried in the exacting conditions of major offensive operations, worthily emulated those of more arduous experience and earned their right to participate in the more difficult task to come. Your staff and auxiliary services, which labored so untiringly and so enthusiastically, deserve equal commendation, and we are indebted to the willing cooperation of veteran French divisions and of auxiliary units which the Allied commands put at our disposal.

Not only did you straighten a dangerous salient, capture 16000 prisoners and 443 guns and liberate 240 square miles of French territory, but you demonstrated the fitness for battle of a unified American Army.

We appreciate the loyal training and effort of the First Army. In the name of our country, I offer our hearty and unmeasured thanks to these splendid Americans of the 1st, 4th and 5th Corps and of the 1st, 2nd, 4th, 5th, 26th, 42nd, 82nd, 89th, and 90th Divisions, which were engaged, and of the 3rd, 35th, 78th, 80th and 91st Divisions, which were in reserve.

This order will be read to all organizations at the first assembly formation after its receipt.

John J. Pershing,
General, Commander-in-Chief.

Official:
Robert C. Davis,
  Adjutant General.

———

Argonne.

<table>
<tr><td>General Order
No. 20.</td><td>Headquarters First Army.
American Expeditionary Forces.
September 28, 1918.</td></tr>
</table>

1. The Allied troops are now engaged all along the Western Front in the largest combined movement of the war. It is of extreme importance that the 1st American Army drive forward with all possible force.

There is evidence that the enemy is retiring from our own front.

Our success must be followed up with the utmost energy, and pursuit continued to bring about the confusion and demoralization, and to prevent the enemy from forming his shattered forces.

I am counting on the splendid spirit, dash and courage of our Army to overcome all opposition. Our country expects nothing else.

John J. Pershing,
General, Commanding First Army.

Official:
Joseph F. Barnes,
Adjutant General.

Advanced Headquarters, First Army Corps,
October 7, 1918.

From: Chief of Staff, 1st Army Corps, U.S.
To: Commanding General, 1st Division.
Subject: Commendation.

1. Under telephonic orders received from 1st Army Headquarters, your command passes temporarily today to the 5th Corps.

2. The Corps Commander directs me to inform you that the work accomplished by your command has come up to the highest expectations and is up to the standard which has long ago been set and always maintained by the Pioneer Division of the American Expeditionary Forces.

By command of Major General Liggett,
Malin Craig,
Chief of Staff.

Headquarters, First Division.
American Expeditionary Forces,
France, October 11, 1918.

1. Pursuant to the orders of the Commander-in-Chief, the undersigned relinquishes command of the 1st Division to assume command of the 5th Army Corps.

2. It is with the feelings of the most profound regret and with a sense of great personal loss that the honor which has come to me in the command of this Division must be interrupted for service in other fields of usefulness. To the officers and enlisted men of the First Division, I extend the most profound gratitude for the loyalty and devotion with which they have answered every call to duty during the great campaigns in which we have participated together. Throughout its service the 1st Division has served as a model not only to the troops of our own land but to the Armies of the world. They have met and defeated the flower of the great Prussian Army, and in every case where duty has called them they have shown themselves worthy of the finest traditions of our great country and of the armies that have made its history brilliant. The history of the 1st Division will form one of the most brilliant pages in the annals of our nation, and through all generations to come those who formed a part of it will associate with pride their participation in its campaigns, and the highest honor that their posterity can enjoy will be that of having an ancestor who shared in the glory of its campaigns.

I have a feeling of certainty that the traditions of this Division will be preserved by all who come after us and that its future will bring even greater victories than those that have distinguished its past. My interest will be continuous and it will be my earnest and constant hope that its successes will contribute in the future as they have in the past to the restoration of the world-peace, and to the maintenance of the lofty ideals for which our country has entered the war.

C. P. Summerall,
Major General, U.S.A.,
Commanding.

The following letter was received from the Commanding General of the 5th Army Corps:

Headquarters, Fifth Army Corps,
American Expeditionary Forces,
France, 30 October 1918.

From: Commanding General, Fifth Army Corps.
To: Commanding General, 1st Field Artillery Brigade.
            (Through Commanding General 1st Division.)
Subject: Commendation.

1. I desire to commend most earnestly the officers and men of the 1st Field Artillery Brigade for the conspicuous devotion to duty, the fine morale exhibited by them and the great assistance that the Brigade has rendered to the Corps during the operations that have been in progress since the relief of the First Division.

2. On account of the need for artillery, this Brigade was retained actively in the Corps front during the period that it was necessary to relieve the rest of the First Division for rest, recruitment and training. In spite of the fact that the personnel. of the 1st Field Artillery Brigade had been without rest during that time, they have rendered services of the highest value and have exhibited a self-sacrificing devotion to duty which is worthy of the First Division and the best traditions of our service. With such troops our future success is assured.

C. P. Summerall,
Major General. Commanding.

1st Ind.

Hdqrs., 1st Division, France, 31 October 1918, — to Commanding General, 1st Field Artillery Brigade, 1st Division.

It is with profound satisfaction that the Commanding General of the First Division forwards this appreciation of the splendid qualities, technical, moral and material, which have consistently characterized the work of the 1st Field Artillery Brigade during its service in this war.

Frank Parker,
Brigadier, General,
Commanding.

Headquarters, Second Division (Regular),
American Expeditionary Forces,
France, November 2, 1918.

From: Commanding General, 2nd Division.
To: Commanding General, 1st Division.
Subject: Expression of Appreciation for Assistance.

1. The success of the attack of the 2nd Division on November 1st, 1918, was largely due to the efficient and energetic cooperation of the 1st Field Artillery Brigade, 1st Division. It is requested that the above mentioned organization be informed of the high appreciation of the 2nd Division of its valuable assistance.

(Signed) John J. Lajeune,
Major General U.S.M.C.

Rec'd. 18:30 November 5, 1918.

Memorandum for Commanding Generals,
1st and 5th Corps.
Subject: Message from the Commander-in-Chief.

1. General Pershing desires that the honor of entering Sedan should fall to the First American Army. He has every confidence that the Troops of the 1st Corps, assisted on their right by the 5th Corps, will enable him to realize his desire.

2. In transmitting the foregoing message, your attention is invited to the favorable opportunity now existing for pressing our advance throughout the night. Boundaries will not be considered binding.

Official: By command of Lieut. General Liggett.
G. C. Marshall Jr.
A. C. of S. G—3.

Headquarters, Fifth Army Corps,
American Expeditionary Forces
France, 10 November, 1918.

From: Commanding General, 5th Army Corps.
To: Commanding General, 1st Division.
Subject: Commendation.

Upon the relief of the 1st Division from service with the 5th Army Corps, I desire to convey to you and to the officers and soldiers of the Division my profound appreciation of the high standards of the maneuvering and fighting power that exists in the Division, and of the energetic and able manner in which the Division responds to every task entrusted to it.

The 1st Division was relieved from this Corps on October 10th after a prolonged and desperate battle in which it suffered unusually heavy casualties. It returned to the rear area, was recruited and trained and was again able to take its place in the lines as a first class combat division on October 30th. As Corps Reserve it followed the operation of this Corps during the advance commenced November 1st, and was placed in line for assault on November 5. The records show that within 48 hours it marched all night for two nights, fought all day for two days and covered at least 60 kilometers across country and through woods, and for the last 10 kilometers in the face of the enemy. By its vigorous and powerful action it drove the enemy across the river as far as Mouzon and made a dash to the hills south of Sedan where it formed preparatory to an assault on that place.

The country may well feel proud of such an organization and all officers and soldiers of the 1st Division may justly cherish the privilege of serving with it during this period of the war.

C. P. Summerall,
Major General, Commanding.

G. H. Q.
American Expeditionary Forces.

General Orders   France, Nov. 19, 1918.
No. 201.

1. The Commander-in-Chief desires to make record in the General Orders of the American Expeditionary Forces his extreme satisfaction with the conduct of the officers and men of the 1st Division in its advance west of the Meuse between October 4th and 11th, 1918. During this period the Division gained a distance of 7 kilometers over a country which presented not only remarkable facilities for enemy defense, but also great difficulties of terrain for the operations of our troops.

2. The Division met with resistance from elements of eight hostile divisions, most of which were first class troops and some of which were completely rested. The enemy chose to defend his position to death, and the fighting was always of the most desperate kind. Throughaut the operations the officers and men of the Division displayed the highest type

of courage, fortitude and self-sacrificing devotion to duty. In addition to many enemy killed, the Division captured 1407 of the enemy, thirteen 77 mm field guns, 10 trench mortars and numerous machine guns and stores.

3. The success of the Division in driving a deep advance into the enemy's territory enabled an assault to be made on the left by the neighboring division against the northeastern portion of the Forest of Argonne and enabled the 1st Division to advance to the right and outflank the enemy's position in front of the division on that flank.

4. The Commander-in-Chief has noted in this Division a special pride of service and a high state of morale, never broken by hardship nor battle.

5. This order will be read to all organizations at the first assembly formation after its receipt.

Official:

Robert C. Davis,
Adjutant General.

By command of General Pershing:

James W. McAndrew,
Chief of Staff.

Headquarters Fifth Army Corps.
American Expeditionary Forces.

General Order   France, 20 November, 1918.
   No. 26.

1. The following citations are announced:

The 1st, 2nd and 89th Divisions, 5th Corps, American E. F., for their part in the memorable attack launched by the 1st American Army on the 1st of November. Throughout this operation all officers and men, by their high courage, devotion to duty and disregard for the innumerable hardships encountered, made themselves a place in the history of our country.

Extract.

"The 1st Division, American E. F., (Brig. General Frank Parker, Commanding), extended the left of the Corps during the advance, after a long and hard march, took up the pursuit of the enemy, marching, fighting day and night with great courage and determination. It added to its already brilliant record by an historical march of two days and nights, arriving on the heights southeast of the city of Sedan."

Official:

Harry C. Kaefring,
Adjutant General.

C. P. Summerall,
Major General, Commanding.

G. H. Q.

American Expeditionary Forces,

General Orders   France, December 19, 1918.
No. 232.

It is with a sense of gratitude for its splendid accomplishments which will live through all history, that I record in General Orders a tribute to the victory of the First Army in the Meuse-Argonne battle.

Tested and strengthened by the reduction of the St. Mihiel salient, for more than six weeks you battered against the pivot of the enemy line on the Western Front. It was a position of imposing natural strength stretching on both sides of the Meuse River from the bitterly contested hills of Verdun to the almost impenetrable forest of the Argonne; a position, moreover, fortified by four years of labor designed to render it impregnable; a position held with the fullest resources of the enemy. That position you broke utterly and thereby hastened the collapse of the enemy's military power.

Soldiers of all the divisions engaged under the 1st, 3rd and 5th American Corps and the 2nd Colonial and 17th French Corps, the 1st, 2nd, 3rd, 4th, 5th, 26th, 28th, 29th, 32nd, 33rd, 35th, 37th, 42nd, 77th, 78th, 79th, 80th, 81st, 82nd, 89th, 90th and 91st American Divisions, the 18th and 26th French Divisions and the 10th and 15th French Colonial Divisions — you will be long remembered for the stubborn persistence of your progress, your storming of obstinately defended machine gun nests, your penetration yard by yard of woods and ravines, your heroic resistance in the face of counter-attacks supported by powerful artillery fire. For more than a month, from the initial attack of September 26th, you fought your way slowly through the Argonne, through the woods and over hills west of the Meuse; you slowly enlarged your hold on the Cotes de Meuse on the east, and then, on the 1st of November, your attack forced the enemy into flight. Pressing his retreat you cleared the entire left bank of the Meuse south of Sedan, and then stormed the heights on the right bank and drove him into the plain beyond.

Soldiers of all Army and Corps troops engaged: to you no less credit is due; your steadfast adherence to duty and your dogged determination in the face of all obstacles made possible the heroic deeds cited above.

The achievement of the 1st Army, which is scarcely to be equaled in American history, must remain a source of proud satisfaction to the troops who participated in the last campaign of the war. The American people will remember it as a realization of the hitherto potential strength of the American contribution to the cause to which they had sworn allegiance. There can be no greater reward for a soldier or for a soldier's memory.

This order will be read to all organizations at the first assembly formation after its receipt.

John J. Pershing,
General, Commander-in-Chief,
American Expeditionary Forces.

Official:
Robert C. Davis,
Adjutant General.

After the Armistice.

G. H. Q.

American Expeditionary Forces.

General Order   France, November 12, 1918.
No. 203.

The enemy has capitulated. It is fitting that I address myself in thanks directly to the officers and men of the American Expeditionary Forces, who, by their heroic efforts, have made possible this glorious result. Our Armies, hurriedly and hastily trained, met a veteran enemy, and by courage, discipline and skill always defeated him. Without complaint you have endured incessant toil, privation and danger. You have seen many of your comrades make the supreme sacrifices that freedom may live. I thank you for the patience and courage with which you have endured. I congratulate you upon the splendid fruits of victory which your heroism and the blood of our gallant dead are now presenting to our nation. Your deeds will live forever on the most glorious pages of America's history.

Those things you have done. There remains now a harder task which will test your soldierly qualities to the utmost. Succeed in this and little note will be taken and few praises will be sung; fail, and the light of your glorious achievements of the past will sadly be dimmed. But you will not fail. Every natural tendency may urge towards relaxation in discipline, in conduct, in appearance, in everything that marks the soldier. Yet you will remember that each officer and each soldier is the representative in Europe of his people and that his brilliant deeds of yesterday permit no action of today to pass unnoticed by friend or foe. You will meet this test as gallantly as you have met the tests of the battle field. Sustained by your high ideals and inspired by the heroic part you have played, you will carry back to your people the proud consciousness of a new Americanism born of sacrifice.

Whether you stand on hostile territory or on the friendly soil of France, you will so bear yourselves in discipline, appearance and respect for civil rights that you will confirm for all time the pride and love which every American feels for your uniform and for you.

Official:

Robert C. Davis,
Adjutant General.

John J. Pershing,
General, Commander-in-Chief.

G. H. Q.
American Expeditionary Forces.

General Order
No. 204.

France, November 12, 1918.

The following proclamation from the Commander-in-Chief of the Allied Armies is published to the Command:

G. H. Q., 12 November 1918.

Officers, Non-Commissioned Officers, Soldiers of the Allied Armies: —

After having resolutely stopped the enemy, you have continuously attacked him for months with a confidence and an energy that never slackened.

You have won the greatest battle of history, and saved the most sacred cause. — the Liberty of the World.

Be proud of the immortal glory with which you have crowned your flags.

Posterity keeps for you her gratitude.

F. Foch,
Marshal of France.
Commander-in-Chief of the Allied Armies.

Official:

Robert C. Davis,
Adjutant General.

By command of General Pershing:
James W. McAndrew,
Chief of Staff.

Headquarters, First Division,
American Expeditionary Forces,
France, November 19, 1918.

From: Commanding General, 1st Division,
To: Commanding General, 1st Field Artillery Brigade.
Subject: Commendation.

1. Upon relinquishing command of the 1st Division, the Commanding General desires to express to you and through you to the officers, non-commissioned officers and

men of your command his deep admiration for your splendid Brigade which throughout this war has merited the complete confidence and deepest respect of this Division.

2. Having commanded the first regiment (Infantry) in line of this Division, the 1st Brigade and the 1st Division successively throughout this war, I have had ample opportunities to observe the work of the 1st Field Artillery Brigade in all its phases and campaigns. The Infantry of this Division has, from the start, had the most complete confidence in its Artillery, a confidence which has increased with each succeeding combat and operation until the signing of Armistice on the 11th day of November 1918. To this confidence has been added an ever increasing respect and affection until the close of the war has found the Infantry and Artillery of the 1st Division bound closely together, each with a thorough sympathy, respect and understanding of the other.

This document will convey to your command a testimonial from the Infantry of this Division to the effect that you have at all times merited the confidence of the Infantry, — no higher praise can be given.

4. Your Brigade has been at all times conspicuous as a type of the military character which has made the record of the 1st Division during the war.

5. I request that you read this testimonial in person to your officers assembled and that you request them in turn to have it read in such a manner that every one of the 1st Field Artillery Brigade may realize the profound respect and admiration of the Division Commander for your Brigade which so well typifies the character of the 1st Division of the American Expeditionary Forces.

(signed): Frank Parker,
Brigadier General, Commanding.

General Orders:
No. 28.

Headquarters First Division.
American Expeditionary Forces.
Montabaur, Germany, 18 March 1919.

The Division Commander desires to express to the Division at large his proud appreciation of its conduct, appearance and steady improvement during the past four months. Particularly he acknowledges the splendid appearance of the Division at the review for the Commander-in-Chief on the 14th instant, and for the soldierly bearing of individuals and of units throughout the Division.

The Commander-in-Chief; the Commanding General, 3rd Army; the Commanding General, 3rd Corps and numerous visitors, military and civilian, have spoken in words of highest praise regarding that ceremony. Officers of the Division have visited the reviews of other troops of the 3rd Army and have reported that in comparison with them the review of the Division was most beautifully set and executed.

The Division Commander has noted in the areas of divisions on the other side of the Rhine the adoption of methods first put in effect in our own area. He appeals to the pride of the men and officers of the Division to maintain its high standard so that it shall stand first in all good things as in its numerical designation, and he extends to them all his most cordial thanks for the successful efforts which they have already made.

This order will be read at the first Retreat formation following its receipt and will be posted on all bulletin boards.

By command of Major General McGlachlin:

Stephen O. Fuqua,

Colonel, General Staff,
Chief of Staff.

American Expeditionary Forces.
Office of the Commander-in-Chief.

France, March 26th, 1919.

Major General Edward F. McGlachlin, Jr.,
Commanding, First Division,
American E. F.

My dear General McGlachlin:

To the officers and men of the 1st Division, I wish to express my compliments upon their excellent appearance at the inspection and review on March 14th at Montabaur. The high morale of all ranks and the condition of the artillery and transportation were what one might expect to find in a command with such a splendid fighting record. The 1st Division has the distinction of having been the first combatant unit to arrive in France and the first to enter the fighting line. From that time until the present its work has been marked by a high state of excellence and efficiency.

After serving in the Somerviller and Ansauville Sectors, the Division entered the line near Montdidier, and on May 28th took Cantigny. This attack may be considered as

the beginning of American offensive operations, and its
success had much to do with the creation of the splendid
spirit thereafter displayed by the American troops. In the
Aisne-Marne offensive, the Division participated in some of
the most desperate fighting of the entire war, and helped
to insure the success of the Allied attack. During the early
part of August the Division moved to the Saizerais Sector,
and shortly after took part in the St. Mihiel operation, making
a deep advance through the Rupt de Mad, across the
Vigneulles-St. Benoid road to Hatton-Chattel. In the Meuse-
Argonne battle the Division was twice thrown into the
line, — on October 1st, at which time it pushed forward in
spite of heavo resistance, and on November 5th, when, after
a march of 20 kilometers to reach the jumping-off line,
it attacked the enemy and marched on Sedan.

Since the signing of the Armistice, the 1st Division, as
a part of the Army of Occupation, has had the honor in
safeguarding the results of its victories, and for its conduct
in this work I have only praise and commendation. In view
of the abve record, each man in the Division should feel
an especial pride in its accomplishments, and I want all
ranks to know my appreciation of the achievements which
stand to their credit, and of the admiration in which they
are held by their fellows throughout the American Expeditionary Forces.

Sincerely yours,

(Signed): John J. Pershing.

Through the medium of the Division newspaper, the
Bridgehead Sentinel, the Commanding General, E. F. McGlachlin
Jr., delivered at different times the fyllowing messages:

The first appeared on the occasion of the Horse Shyw.

General McGlachlin to the First Division:

Men of the First Division:

Every man in the best company!
Every company in the best battalion!
Every battalion in the best regiment!
Every regiment in the best brigade!
All of us in the best division!

And our Division a part of the finest great soldier-
body in the world.

That is the way I wish that we may feel.

To feel so, each of us must do his best, for then
only, can he be proud of himself and proud of his comrades.

Our Horse Show is held so that we may see the results of one another's efforts, benefit by what is good, take heed of what is bad. By it we shall select some, not necessarily all, of those who are to represent us in comparison with other divisions. The awards will indicate, in part, whether each of us does actually belong to the best organization. If we do we must continue to keep ahead. If we do not we must press on to overtake those who have done better. I would like to see the Division a winner in everything. It is quite possible to make its animal transport a continuous Horse-Show, — to make the eye glad, the heart proud and other divisions envious. I know that you can do this, for I know well your courage and gallantry, your high fighting spirit, your splendid health and your firm determination.

(Signed): E. F. McGlachlin Jr.

The Second Message, April 20, 1919.

To the Division:

Undying fame is gained by and rests firmly with that division which, distinguished by courage and gallantry in action, by efficiency in operations, inflicts depressing losses on the foe, sustains its own with fortitude, absorbs replacements rapidly with maintenance of morale, is marked by unfaltering determination to win.

Though a division's fame may be glorious and widely established, it is quite possible for its reputation to decline. It cannot live in the past but must march straight in the present with a steady forward gaze.

As each of us shares in the benefits of this Division, each of us owes it the duty of maintaining its splendid traditions and of being worthy always of its wonderful accomplishments. As our comrades before have won its fame by unsurpassable heroism, it must be our unalterable purpose now to secure its reputation by soldierly conduct, high character, good carriage, splendid appearance and fine courtesy. It is only by being simple, thorough and direct and, even in small things, by holding high standards of duty, by ever thinking of our honor and that of our Division, by unfailing love of our country that we may keep the First Division worthy of its imperishable fame already gained.

E. F. McGlachlin Jr.,
Major General, U. S. Army,
Commanding.

To the Division:

The Third Message, May 3, 1919.

Two former classmates of mine, now large employers in civil life, told me that they sought men who have served in the Army because they found them to be more alert, obedient, loyal and physically able than those without military training. But they said they scrutinized the discharge certificates very carefully.

Before the war there were very few employers who knew the value of the discharge certificate as evidence of character. Now there are thousands who have actually prepared them and thoroughly know their importance. All commanders have been directed to display the Form for Honorable Discharge on bulletin boards.

I appeal to every man to keep his record clean. An examination of court martial cases shows many instances of men who have long served without trial until a moment's weakness, discouragement or indifference led to the departure from the high standards of discipline that the Division has always held and to some act which has placed a blot on their military records.

When it is considered that the discharge certificate which a great many will receive in a few months is not only a record of past service but is possibly the key to future success in the Army or out of it, care should be taken that no record of conviction or of disciplinary action shall mar its excellence.

The Division has done big things and we must live up to them in a big way. This requires firmness and courage but it is well worth the effort. Let the men of the First Division by their conduct reduce to nothing the necessity for courtmartial and disciplinary action.

Keep your record clean.

E. F. McGlachlin, Jr.,
Major General, U. S. Army,
Commanding.

The Fourth Message, June 7, 1919.

To the Division.

German eyes look and see, Boche ears listen and hear, Hun lips tell all the half-truths and lies and only those truths calculated to accomplish their particular selfish objects.

Our enemy still attempts always to impose his ideas on the world.

Given every opportunity to avoid the war, he insists that he was not responsible.

Beaten by Allied arms under American impetus, he denies that he was defeated but claims that he was deceived.

Entering Belgium contrary to sacred promise, he avers, untruthfully, that a hostile nation did so first.

Determined at the beginning to force his will upon all peoples not only for the power and grandeur and enrichment of Germany but for the fatal impoverishment of other nations, at the height of his successes he announced a pitiless policy of punishment of those who were fighting against him. Far beyond the requirements of military necessity, he killed American women and children through his underseas piracy, killed and maimed English women and children through bombardment of undefended places, destroyed French mines beyond repair for fifteen years and ruined and stole Belgian machinery for no purpose except to delay resumption of industry that his own might more greatly prosper.

Having through greed inficted infinite losses upon us and our Allies he now whines and weeps and wrings his hands that he is called upon for reparation in kind, though not in measure, for his misdeeds. He cries out against the diminution of warpower imposed upon him to remove his serious menace to peace, not to punish him.

As during the war by bribery, corruption, spying, stealth, secret destruction, lies, theft, violence, murder, violation of women, slavery, cruelty to children and old men and women he made himself the horror of the world, now by his insolence, bluff, lies, appeals for sympathy he makes himself contemptible. Contemptible, his might is no longer to be feared though he is dangerous. He is dangerous because without conscience he conducts an organized unscrupulous campaign to deny his unmeasured crimes, to create mutual distrust between the Allies, to make us suspicious of each other, to plant in our minds seeds of doubt of our principles, our institutions and our President, to gain sympathy for his future imaginary distress.

In that organized campaign the people among whom, through necessity, we live play their parts. By little welcome favors, by insistence, by repetition, by making a friend here and another there they attempt to force their wedges of argument, disclaim, pleading, suspicion and distrust to break our conviction in the righteousness of our cause, the unworthiness of theirs.

There is nothing consistent between German public motive and American spirit and ideals. There is nothing in our soldierly duty requiring or authorizing us to convert our enemy to our beliefs. There is everything in our soldierly duty requiring us to keep faithfully our own beliefs, to be loyal to our Allies and to sustain our American traditions and morale.

Let us see everything, hear everything, of value to our cause, say nothing to our enemy. Let us present and maintain our honor, perform exactly our duty, devote ourselves loyally to our country.

E. F. McGlachlin, Jr.
Major General U. S. A. Commanding.

Headquarters Third Army Corps
American Expeditionary Forces
Office of Commanding General.

General Orders   June 26, 1919.
No. 51.

1. The Corps Commander desires to congratulate the officers and men of the command upon the announced intentions of the Germans to sign the Peace Treaty, and hence 'the victorious termination of the great war, in which you have played so conspicuous a part.

2. The promptness and resolution of your recent concentration for a further advance was the final and conclusive proof to our enemies that you intended to see the work you had so well begun successfully concluded before you stopped. This was the deciding factor in causing them to realize that further resistance was hopeless, and that in spite of their protests their signature must be affixed to the peace terms of the Allies.

3. There remains for you, therefore, in the probably short interim before your return to the United States, by the orderliness of your behavior and the temperance of your conduct, to hold yourselves prepared for that return and leave untarnished, in the last days of your occupation of the Rhineland, the splendid reputation you have earned as soldiers on the battlefields and as men in the trying months of the long armistice.

4. Organization Commanders will read this order to their commands at the first practicable formation after its receipt.

Official:

David O'Keefe,
Adjutant General.

Dist. "C".

J. L. Hines,
Major General, U. S. A.
Commanding.

Headquarters Third Army
American Expeditionary Forces.

General Order   2 July, 1919.
  No. 62.

    1: The following is published for the information of the Command:

Chaumont, 2 July 1919.

From: Lieutenant General Hunter Liggett, U. S. Army.
To: Chief of Staff, Third Army.
Subject: Dissolution of the Third Army.

    1. I am informed that orders will issue this date dissolving the Third Army and returning me to the United States.

    2. I desire to record my official satisfaction and personal gratification at having commanded the splendid units constituting the Third Army and further my sincere regret at leaving the officers and men who have made the Third Army, upheld its standard, and who, by their reliability and steadfast attention to the duties devolved upon them, caused that Army and its accomplishments to pass into history with the proudest and fairest of records.

    3. To the wonderful Military Machine which constitutes my Staff, I desire to give special thanks. The officers and men of that Staff tried out in the earlier days in the A. E. F. constitute a picture of efficiency, ability, and loyalty which will always remain with me, and I face the final years of my active military career with the sincere thanks and the utmost satisfaction that I have known such men and have enjoyed them as friends and companions.

Official: H. Liggett.
Malin Craig,   Lieut. General,
Chief of Staff.   Commanding Third Army.

Headquarters First Division,
American Forces in Germany,
Montabaur, Germany, 9 July 1919.

General Orders
  Number 59.

    In its march to the Rhine, its occupation of the Coblenz Bridgehead, its preparation for further fighting, its concentration for rapid advance, the Division has called forth expressions of praise and admiration from Corps and Army Commanders. It has sustained well its former reputation gained in battle.

With the ratification to-day of Peace by the German National Assembly at Weimar its immediate experience of war comes to a close.

Its rank and file have been simple, direct and thorough; gallant, determined and efficient; loyal, patriotic and temperate; good-humored, severe and just.

From now there will be rapid and great changes in its personnel. Before so many comrades leave us and at the real conclusion of the war the Commanding General thanks every officer and man for his services and for these splendid qualities which have shown to the world what a fine thing an American division may become.

The First Division is a living personality to inspire love and respect in all of us, whether we remain with it or pass to other duties and responsibilities in military or civil life.

E. F. McGlachlin, Jr.,
Major General, U. S. Army,
Commanding.

Extract

.... from speech delivered by General Pershing at London, July 17, 1919.

You will recall that when our 1st Division entered the battle line and fought the small though brilliant battle — the first as an independent command — at Cantigny, that the success which attended the attack not only set an example for future American divisions to follow, but really had an electrifying effect through the Allied lines and gave new hope to the armies.

"The Armistice stopped the First Division once; the signing of Peace stopped it a second time; German soldiers never stopped it."

Edwin L. James,
War Correspondent,
"New York Times".